QUICK FIXES

Fuel Economy

Publications International, Ltd.

Photo credits:

Front cover: **Getty Images** (left)

American Honda Motor Company: 55, 64; **Brand X Pictures:** 51; **Chrysler LLC:** 58, 63; **Dreamstime:** Eraxion, 66; Picturelake, 7; **Ford Motor Company:** 44, 59; **General Motors Corporation:** 60, 62; **Hyundai Motor America:** 54; **iStockphoto:** 29, 31; **Kia Motors Corporation:** 56; **Mazda North American Operations:** 57; **Mercedes-Benz USA:** 61; **PhotoDisc:** 8; **Shutterstock:** 4, 11, 15, 16, 20, 23, 24, 28, 33, 34, 43, 49, 78; **Toyota Motor-Sales, USA:** 47, 65

Copyright © 2008 Publications International, Ltd. All rights reserved. This publication may not be reproduced or quoted in whole or in part by any means whatsoever without written permission from:

Louis Weber, CEO
Publications International, Ltd.
7373 North Cicero Avenue
Lincolnwood, Illinois 60712

Permission is never granted for commercial purposes.

ISBN-13: 978-1-4127-0440-3
ISBN-10: 1-4127-0440-5

Manufactured in USA

8 7 6 5 4 3 2 1

CONTENTS

INTRODUCTION:

Saving Fuel = Money in Your Pocket   4

If you'd like to save money on gas, this book is for you. Most of the timely tips in these pages will help whether you drive a thousand miles a week or never cover that much distance in a month.

CHAPTER ONE:

Think Economically   21

Small changes can result in substantial savings in gas and money. Some of the best fuel-saving techniques are also the easiest.

CHAPTER TWO:

Drive Economically   28

Good drivers are smooth drivers, and smooth driving saves fuel. Even minor adjustments in how you drive can result in substantial savings in gas and money.

CHAPTER THREE:

SUVs and MPG   44

Buoyed in great measure by affordable fuel, America in the 1990s turned its automotive appetite to light trucks. The category includes pickups, minivans, and the models that experienced the fastest-rising popularity of all—sport-utility vehicles. Plus, our picks for the most fuel-efficient vehicles in the following classes: subcompact, compact, midsize, and large cars; compact, midsize, and large SUVs; minivan; pickup truck; and hybrid.

INTRODUCTION
SAVING FUEL = MONEY IN YOUR POCKET

If you'd like to save money on gas, this book is for you. Most of the timely tips in these pages will help whether you drive a thousand miles a week or never cover that much distance in a month, whether you drive a subcompact, a hybrid, a sports car, or a sport-utility vehicle, whether you agonize daily in rush-hour traffic or seldom stray from open rural highways.

Much of driving economically is a matter of unlearning a few bad habits and substituting some good ones. We've all been warned about "jackrabbit" starts, for instance, and speeding. Such actions are dangerous as well as wasteful, yet we see them all the time.

Saving gas is like getting a raise; it means more money in your pocket.

The trouble is, many of us learned to drive at a time when economy was not a high priority and when cars weren't built with thrift in mind. Even the basics of scheduled maintenance were mainly for the purpose of boosting performance, not for adding extra miles per gallon.

Americans seldom gave much thought to fuel economy before the Arab Oil Embargo of 1973. The specter of long gas-station lines, unreliable supply, and fluctuating prices reared again with the fuel crisis of 1979–80. Those events were wake-up calls, and Detroit and Asian automakers responded with lots of gas-sipping compacts. But by the late 1980s, horsepower and performance were back in vogue.

Average fuel economy for passengers cars, after rising steadily for more than a decade, began to decline by 1989. Cars were getting faster, more powerful, more laden with gadgetry—and gulping more fuel. Americans had evidently decided, perhaps unknowingly, that a new crisis wasn't going to happen. The popularity of light trucks, notably sport-utility vehicles and pickup trucks, grew very quickly in the late eighties, when Ford's F-150 pickup became the best-selling vehicle in America. Trendy was spelled "SUV."

In short, life on the American road was good. We were paying far less for our automotive fun than were motorists in most European countries—just as we had for decades. Adjusted for inflation, motor fuel costs in the late eighties had reached their lowest point since the years just after World War II.

Then, in August 1990, Iraq invaded Kuwait. Within a week, the average price of gasoline shot up more than 16 cents a gallon. A month later, prices stabilized somewhat, though at a level some 30 cents higher than before the crisis. Suddenly, government officials issued stern warnings about the need for frugality. Polls suggested that many Ameri-

> **What This Book Can Do For You**
>
> **This book has three goals:**
>
> **1.** To explain how you can get the best fuel economy from your present vehicle, whether an economy car, a luxury sedan, SUV, or pickup. This means taking a look at how you drive, where you drive, and how you make use of options and accessories that drain away more fuel than many of us realize.
>
> **2.** To describe the essential steps of basic preventive maintenance, some of which you can still do yourself. Not only will these simple actions help eke out more miles per gallon, they'll extend the life of your car, so you're saving money over the long haul as well as the short term. In addition, scheduled maintenance helps make sure your engine is emitting its minimal potential of pollutants into the atmosphere.
>
> **3.** To help you make a fuel-minded decision when buying your next vehicle, whether it's to be purchased new or secondhand.

cans would return to fuel-sipping cars if gas prices reached $1.40 a gallon. More than half claimed they would do so if prices hit $2.00. Many simply said they already were cutting back on driving.

Of course, the modern downsized automobile was already far more frugal than its elephantine ancestors. The average new passenger car achieved 27.8 miles per gallon in 1990. Sure, that was down from a high of 28.6 mpg in 1988, but it was still far thriftier than the 14.2-mpg average of 1974. Maybe America was on the right track after all.

SUVs and other light trucks

Things were also changing at the high-mileage end of the fuel-consumption spectrum. Gas-sipping imports, which had played a major role in redirecting the industry during the 1970s, weren't quite so thrifty anymore. Japanese automakers were veering away from the subcompact market in which they'd gained their reputations. Instead, they'd moved upscale, turning to handsome but thirsty performance and luxury models, such as the Infiniti and Lexus sedans introduced for 1990.

By that time, barely 3 percent of shoppers were driving off in cars that yielded 40 mpg or more. About 30 percent of cars available in 1990 offered mileage of more than 30 mpg, but few Americans seemed to care.

The time period marked a high point in America's love affair with the SUV, which was prized for its commanding view of the road, presumed safety, and luxury image. And many SUVs, like many pickups, had the added allure of four-wheel drive—a system that eats up more gas than two-wheel drive.

SUV sales skyrocketed in the early nineties, and by the end of the decade virtually every automaker that maintained a presence in the U.S. offered one or more sport-utes—even Porsche. There was an SUV or pickup for every budget, demographic, and attitude.

SUVs put a serious hurt on production of more economical station wagons and stole sales from generally more fuel-efficient minivans.

Global trouble, domestic disaster

The terrorist attacks of September 11, 2001, initiated a gradual but steady climb in prices at the pump, which accelerated after America's spring 2003 invasion of Iraq. As with any war, combat costs soon made their way back to the folks at home.

The $2.00-per-gallon barrier was shattered in 2004, but prices didn't stop there. Iraqi oil production was crippled by the war, and American demand for gas—360 million gallons every day—continued unabated.

But in 2005 the per-barrel price for crude oil jumped to $50 on the world market, startling economists and other analysts. Pump prices rose. Then came $60 a barrel: pump prices continued to rise. Then $70 a barrel. Average cost of a gallon of gas in the U.S. at the end of summer 2005 approached $3.00 a gallon, a figure exceeded in many urban areas. Every oil-producing country save Saudi Arabia was producing at full capacity. We wanted more oil, but it wasn't going to

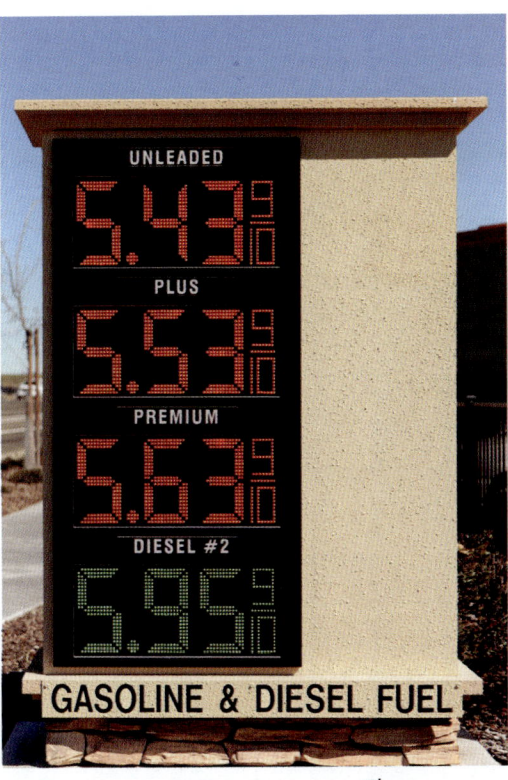

The national-average price of gasoline has doubled since 2004.

come easily. President Bush authorized use of the nation's Strategic Petroleum Reserve to help keep pump prices in check. Europe, too, released some of its reserves into the world market.

At the end of August 2005, Hurricane Katrina wreaked havoc on the city of New Orleans and badly damaged nearby oil refineries and port facilities vital to America's fuel interests. Because the disaster prompted oil companies to increase the wholesale gas price charged to station owners, pump prices in the days following Katrina rose quickly: by 10, 20, 30 cents, and more, in single leaps. Some Midwestern stations exploited customers with pump prices closer to $4.00; in the South, some motorists paid as much as $6.00 a gallon.

When the federal government declared a prohibition on price gouging, the most egregious pump prices declined.

Half the oil processed in the U.S. becomes gasoline. Most of the rest ends up as diesel fuel.

But underground tanks at a few independent stations ran dry, and drivers began to worry that big-oil stations might suffer similar shortfalls. By September 2005, some experts looked to the near future and saw an average pump price of $4 a gallon, perhaps higher.

That future would arrive in 2008, when oil cracked the $100-per-barrel mark for the first time. Paying $4.00 a gallon for gasoline was no longer a distant threat, but a painful reality.

How much gasoline can you save by following all the advice in this book? Ten to 15 percent, maybe more. It depends on the type of car you have, how economical it is to start with, and how carefully you drive already.

So, ladies and gentlemen, let's start our engines—keeping a light foot on the gas pedal, of course—and embark on the road to mmpg (*more* miles per gallon). Then, maybe we can look forward to the time when people start to boast about their gas mileage as much as their 0–60 mph times.

A note on figures in this book

Most mileage estimates come from tests made by the U.S. Environmental Protection Agency (EPA), as part of its emissions-testing program. EPA figures apply to specific car models, predicting how economically they perform in either city or highway driving. The government's Corporate Average Fuel Economy (CAFE) mileage figures are entirely different, referring to the average economy of all models sold by a company.

Some gasoline-price data comes from Zfacts.com and About.com.

CHAPTER ONE
THINK ECONOMICALLY

Small changes can result in substantial savings in gas and money. Some of the best fuel-saving techniques are also the easiest.

- Start by determining whether it's necessary to get in the car and drive.

- If it is, think about your most efficient route.

- Prepare and maintain your car to get the best mileage.

IS THAT DRIVE NECESSARY?

Explore alternative forms of transportation

In a society that values private transportation, going without a car sounds like heresy. Yet surprising numbers of people do exactly that—especially those who live in urban areas. Walking, after all, is excellent exercise and costs absolutely nothing.

Most cities have better bus service than many non-riders may realize. And in some urban areas, commuter rail service efficiently moves thousands to and from work each day. You'll give up some travel-time flexibility, of course, but the duration of your commute may shrink, and you'll be free from the burden of locating and paying for in-town parking.

Lifelong rush-hour motorists may be amazed to discover it can be relaxing to sit back on the bus or commuter train and read or doze. Train and bus schedules are readily avail-

able, both at stations and online. If you can't see giving up the car commute entirely, how about taking mass transit once or twice a week?

Don't overlook the possibility of riding a bicycle instead of traveling by car. It's fine exercise. You won't have parking hassles. Many cities have dedicated bike lanes. And in rush-hour congestion, you may find the maneuverability of a bike allows you to travel more quickly than by car. Approach this alternative with due caution, of course. The right bike, proper safety attire, and a defensive-riding mind-set are essential.

A moped or motorcycle won't free you from all of the costs or burdens of motorized travel. But they afford many of the same advantages as a bicycle, with the obvious ability to go faster and cover longer distances. Or course, the right bike,

Sitting in traffic is a leading cause of poor fuel economy. Consider traveling when fewer people are on the road, and explore less-congested routes.

proper safety attire, and a defensive-riding mind-set are essential here, too.

The online advantage

Finding the lowest gas prices in your area is just a mouse-click away. Several Web sites allow you to type in your zip code and view a roster of pump prices for your region. Go to your search engine and just type in "gas prices."

The Web also offers a universe of services from the comfort of your home. Shop online instead of driving to the mall. Bank online instead of idling in a drive-up bank-window line. Conduct research via the Web instead of driving to the library.

Vacation sensibly

Look into holiday spots where the need to drive after you arrive is minimal or nonexistent. Consider a self-contained resort where you'll enjoy a break from the stress of traffic congestion. Visit an exciting big city, where restaurants, shopping, entertainment, and museums are within walking distance.

If you take a driving vacation, do a little research on attractions close to home. You might have overlooked some great destinations.

Whether traveling near or far, start out when traffic is light. Plan meals and rest stops to blend with peak traffic times in the area. No point in having to feel like a commuter when you're on vacation.

Car pool

Share the ride, share the costs. Talk with neighbors and co-workers about car-pool opportunities, even for just a couple of days a week. You'll save on gas, parking, even wear and tear on the car that gets to skip a day or two of stop-and-go driving.

You'll save time, too. Many highway systems around big cities have car-pool lanes, otherwise known as High Occupancy Vehicle lanes, dedicated to vehicles carrying more than one occupant. While the regular lanes are clogged with crawling peak-travel-time traffic, the HOV lanes are flowing freely. In rural areas, lots may be set aside as car-pool gathering points near a freeway on-ramp.

PLAN YOUR ROUTE

Become your own traffic manager

Planning and modifying where you drive and how you get there can make a big difference in the number of times you have to stop for fuel every week.

What's the point of leaving the house half a dozen times in the course of a day when a little planning will allow you to do everything in one or two trips? Particularly in winter, short trips are hard on an engine, which might never warm up fully. Cold engines guzzle a lot more fuel than properly warmed-up engines.

Drive to the farthest locale first, so the engine warms up completely before you shut it off. Stop-and-go driving with a cold engine puts an even greater strain on its innards.

Drivers who use their cars for business can also learn to plan their trips for the shortest total distance and greatest efficiency. So can families planning play dates and school activities.

The multi-car family advantage

Survey the vehicles available to you and your family and choose the one that's most fuel-efficient. Why take the luxury dreamboat or heavyweight SUV on a quick trek to the supermarket when you could slip into your subcompact instead?

Another way to save fuel is to take the vehicle that's been driven most recently. Engines are grossly inefficient when cold. Startups are hard on the car and can cut drastically into fuel mileage for the first few miles. All the more so in cold weather. If you have at your disposal a vehicle whose engine isn't stone-cold, consider that one for your errand.

Investigate alternative routes

It's easy to get into a rut, taking the same route day after day, never pondering an alternate that might prove more economical—and even more pleasant.

Experimenting pays. It won't hurt to study a map of the region you travel daily. Consider the number of stoplights along the way, the extent of traffic jams and slowdowns. Use your odometer to measure the distance covered by each route.

Sometimes, it's even wise to travel a little farther if that avoids excess traffic. Whenever feasible, focus on highway travel rather than stop-and-go city routes. Avoid routes that pass through school zones, or follow school bus pickup points, which means slowing to uneconomical speed and perhaps stopping frequently.

Drive when others are not

Plan your time so you're traveling when most other people are not. Ask your employer about flexible work hours that keep you out of the stop-and-go morning and evening rush. Run errands at mid-day rather than 8 a.m. or 4:30 p.m.

Off-peak travel saves fuel and aggravation. Leave rush hour to those who have no choice in the matter.

Drive where others are not

Take the low-traffic alternative. Travel where congestion is least and you can maintain the steadiest speed. When possible, choose smooth, straight, uncongested highways.

In the city, look for through streets with a minimum of stoplights. You might think you're saving time by darting down side streets and alleys in rush hour, but you're more likely to be wasting fuel from all the start-and-stop motion.

Tune in to local radio and TV for up-to-the-minute reports on traffic conditions and accidents. Staying tuned is most vital in bad weather.

Weather makes a difference

Naturally, you can't change the weather, but the fact is you'll burn considerably less fuel driving when the temperature is 70 degrees versus 20 degrees. In cold weather, travel in daylight rather than at night when it's chillier.

Foul weather can be a major detriment to good fuel economy.

Wind also makes a big difference. A strong headwind, even a crosswind, cuts mileage drastically, as your engine fights its way forward. A tailwind can do the opposite, of course.

Heavy rain and snow also cut down on gas mileage, as well as making the travel experience less pleasant. So if you must drive in stormy weather, slow down when the wind is not at your back.

Dress right

Running accessories burns more fuel. Keep that coat zipped and turn the heater blower down a notch or two.

In warm weather, dress lightly to minimize use of the air conditioner until absolutely necessary.

Even opening the windows creates aerodynamic drag, so proper dress can help you regulate your body temperature to stay comfortable and save fuel.

PREPARE YOUR VEHICLE

Tires: A vital consideration

Proper tire inflation is critical to fuel economy, and to safety.

Under-inflated tires cause vehicle "drag" and increase fuel consumption. They also compromise handling ability in turns and in emergency maneuvers. They increase stopping distances and decrease control under braking. Under-inflation puts undue stress on tire sidewalls and also causes rolling tires to rapidly build and retain heat. Stress and heat are prime contributors to tire failure, including blow-outs at high speed. Under-inflated tires also wear down more quickly.

This $3.00 tire gauge can save you $50 to $100 a year.

Properly inflated tires are harder and roll more easily. That helps fuel economy and improves tire life. It allows the treads to grip as designed in all conditions, including rain and snow. And properly inflated tires are able to work with your vehicle's suspension to provide maximum handling, steering, and braking ability.

An estimated four out of ten vehicles on the road have at least one under-inflated tire. Pressure that's 3 pounds per square inch (psi) below the recommended reading may hurt gas mileage by 1.5 percent. Some experts suggest even greater penalties. The Environmental Protection Agency warns that running tires at 20 psi can easily cost you a full mile per gallon.

Proper tire inflation

Tires can naturally lose up to 1 psi every 30 days and will lose pressure more quickly in cold weather. Because cooler air is more dense, pressure drops by about 1 psi for every 10 degrees. A tire inflated to 30 psi at 70 degrees could drop as low as 26 psi at the freezing point.

The recommended tire pressure is displayed in your vehicle, typically on a sticker inside the glovebox door or on one of the doorposts. It's also in your owner's manual. Many vehicles are available with several tire sizes, and each size may have its own recommended inflation pressure.

Match the tire size, as listed on the tire sidewall, with that on the sticker or in the owner's manual. Note that the inflation number listed on the tire sidewall itself shows the maximum inflation, not the optimal pressure as determined by the tire maker and the manufacturer of your vehicle.

Checking tire inflation

Check inflation when the tires are cool. That means they have been driven less than a mile or so. Air expands inside a warm tire and you'll get a false reading.

Tire pressure should be checked at least every 30 days. A tire gauge is the old stand-by. But federal regulations require that in 2008, all new cars, SUVs, minivans and pickup trucks be equipped with an under-inflation warning system.

Sensors will monitor tire pressure, and if it falls 25 percent below the recommended inflation, a yellow warning light on the dashboard will illuminate.

The system will save an estimated 120 lives annually and prevent 8,400 injuries per year, according to the National Highway Traffic Safety Administration. NHTSA estimates it will also save drivers up to $35 annually in longer tread life and in fuel costs. Selected 2004 and 2005 models already had such a system. For the 2006 model year, 20 percent of new vehicles were required to have the system, with 70 percent for 2007, and 100 percent for 2008.

Fuel economy varies with tire type

Those all-terrain or off-road tires with their knobby tread look rough and ready and are designed to get you through rocks and mud. They are not designed to promote high gas mileage.

All-season tires have a less friction-producing tread design and therefore roll more freely, to the benefit of fuel economy. They're generally lighter than all-terrain or off-road tires, and less weight means better fuel economy. They're quieter-riding, better-handling, and longer-wearing, too.

Don't carry more than you need

Keep the car as light as reasonably possible. For each 100 pounds of extra weight, gas mileage is reduced by as much as 4 percent. Limit the everyday items in your trunk or cargo area to the bare necessities, which should include some emergency items, such as a small jug of water, flashlight, and maybe a few tools.

Don't haul around what you won't be using. Leave the golf clubs at home until you head for the links. Extra bulk adds fuel-gulping weight, and it can upset your vehicle's normal weight distribution. That will impair handling and can even rob a front-drive car of valuable traction. If you must carry heavy items, try to put a few of them inside the car.

Remove that rack

Wind drag increases fuel consumption. Get rid of anything that disturbs the smooth flow of air over your vehicle's surface. Most roof racks have removable cross members, and some racks can be removed altogether; take it off if it isn't in use. When you do need to carry something on the roof, keep it light and small—both for fuel-saving aerodynamics and to avoid the risk of a top-heavy weight imbalance.

That grille bar and those running boards may make your SUV look rugged, but they add weight and aero drag.

And that bolt-on trunk-lid spoiler that makes you feel fast and furious? It's designed to harness the wind and press your car to the pavement at high speeds. The result is better grip on the road, but this "downforce" is actually artificial weight that hurts fuel economy. Worse, unless you are a racing technician versed in aerodynamics, chances are excellent that your spoiler isn't doing anything more than adding wind drag and weight. That's costing you at the pump, too.

MAINTAIN YOUR VEHICLE

Poor maintenance means poor mileage

Even simple things like dirty air filters, excessive exhaust emissions, and under-inflated tires can combine to reduce fuel economy by 25 percent.

Routine maintenance on a modern vehicle is relatively easy. Electronics and computerized systems mean there's less to tune and that intervals between servicing are surprisingly long. For example, spark plugs that used to need changing every 10,000 miles might go 30,000, or even 50,000 miles.

Regular maintenance pays off every day

Cars that start quickly, run smoothly, and are in good mechanical condition get the best gas mileage. Whatever cuts into performance hurts economy. Scheduled maintenance also helps make parts last longer, so you save money two ways: today in economy, tomorrow in reduced repair costs.

A tune-up can boost fuel economy up to 10 percent, says the Environmental Protection Agency (EPA). On modern fuel-injected cars equipped with computer-controlled powertrain systems, there's actually little to "tune up." Basically, today's tune-up means replacing the spark plugs, although it's also important to perform the kind of preventive maintenance duties described later in this section.

Dirty engine oil will not only cost you at the pump, it can shorten the life of your car.

Follow the schedule

Your owner's manual likely will list two maintenance schedules: one for "ordinary" driving, the other for "severe" or "heavy-duty" use. Each has its own maintenance program and lists the systems to be checked and the work to be done based on both mileage and time between getting your car serviced.

Even if you don't tow a trailer or drive in dusty conditions, your "ordinary" use can fall into the heavy-duty category if you live in a region subjected to very hot or very cold temperatures. Even subjecting your vehicle to frequent short trips counts as more than ordinary use.

When in doubt, err toward the stricter maintenance schedule. It'll pay off in fuel savings weekly and in long-term reliability.

Emissions and fuel economy

Even if your city or state has no emissions inspections program, exhaust emissions should be checked at least yearly. The lower a car's tailpipe emissions, the more efficiently its engine is operating.

Bringing your car's emissions to within specifications can improve gas mileage as much as 15 percent. And your engine will last longer, too. The oxygen sensor is a key part of your emissions system, and some estimates suggest a faulty oxygen sensor can reduce fuel economy by as much as 40 percent.

Under federal law, most emissions controls are under factory warranty for 5 years or 50,000 miles. So some emissions-related repairs may be covered at no cost to you.

Look, listen, and sniff

Be alert for anything odd. Open the hood and look around for loose wires or hoses. Check fluid levels regularly, as described later in this section. Be aware of any sudden drop in fuel economy, unusual noise, or curious odor. Monitor the coolant-temperature gauge, if your vehicle has one. An engine that runs too hot, or too cool, is probably wasting fuel. Take note of any missing, stumbling, pinging, odd noises, hard starting, or significant loss of power.

SIMPLE DO-IT-YOURSELF GAS-SAVING MAINTENANCE

Stay in tune with your car

For economy's sake, you should know a little something about what's going on under the hood. Though undeniably complex and computerized, the principles of engine operation haven't changed as much over the years as many believe. Even if you don't do the work yourself, a bit of knowledge goes a long way when communicating with your mechanic—and in making sure all the scheduled maintenance gets done.

A little knowledge is a good thing

We're not talking manuals with instructions on replacing your transmission. And, for better or worse, modern vehicles don't afford too many do-it-yourself opportunities.

But there are many books, brochures, and DVDs that can help you get some basic insight into the inner workings of your vehicle. Examine before you buy, however, and make sure the source is aimed at your skill level and is current with the systems on your vehicle.

Don't overlook the automaker's shop manual for your car. Though written primarily with factory-authorized mechanics in mind, it contains plenty of useful information to guide the experienced do-it-yourselfer.

Check and change the oil regularly

Oil is the lifeblood of your vehicle's engine and maintaining proper oil levels and fresh oil will help keep your engine healthy and operating most efficiently. That leads to gas savings.

Check the level on the dipstick at least weekly. The oil should be checked with the engine turned off. The best time to get an accurate reading is when the engine is cold and the oil is pooled in the oil pan rather than disbursed throughout the engine's oil passages.

Always use the correct oil viscosity, as outlined in your owner's manual. The viscosity is described as 5W30 or 10W40, for example, and is a measurement of the oil blend's ability to do its job within a particular range of conditions and temperatures. Using the incorrect viscosity can actually lower fuel economy by up to 2 percent.

Any oil that carries an American Petroleum Institute (API) certification is appropriate. The API also monitors for friction-reducing additives and applies the term "Energy Conserving" to its performance symbol on motor oils that meet this standard.

Some synthetic motor oils are advertised as promoting fuel savings, though the advantage is generally negligible versus simply changing your oil and filter regularly. Some tests have shown that synthetic oils result in slightly improved fuel economy, though their primary purpose is for use in high-performance engines as part of the total performance package. Synthetic oils are quite a bit more expensive than regular oil.

It's become fashionable to change your engine's oil and oil filter every 3,000 miles. It won't hurt to keep to that schedule, though evidence that it's a bit of overkill is in every owner's manual. That's where your vehicle's manufacturer typically specifies 15,000 miles or so between oil changes. They built the engine and should know what it needs to stay in top shape.

You'll save money by not skimping on motor oil. "Energy conserving" oil is worth any added cost.

Replacing a dirty air filter is easy, inexpensive, and will improve your fuel economy.

Some vehicles even have an oil-life monitor that will announce via a dashboard light when an oil change is necessary. These keep track of how the vehicle is driven between oil changes and calculates useful oil life.

Be it outlined in the owner's manual or announced on a dashboard light, we recommend following the manufacturer's oil-change schedule.

Change the air filter

Some experts say not to expect a huge mileage boost from keeping your engine's air filter fresh, while others say a clogged air filter can reduce gas mileage as much as 10 percent.

In any case, changing an air filter is a simple task you can perform, and a properly operating air filter is essential to keeping the engine clean inside. A clogged or really dirty air filter cuts off air to the engine, and there's no doubt that hurts performance and fuel economy.

The cooling system

An engine that runs too cool or too hot may waste 10 to 15 percent of the fuel you put into your gas tank. Your engine's operating temperature is governed primarily by the coolant fluid and the engine's thermostat.

Coolant isn't just water, but a blend of antifreeze and water, and helps maintain proper engine temperature in both hot and cold weather conditions. The proper coolant blend is usually a 50–50 mix of antifreeze and water. The level should be maintained as indicated on the underhood reservoir, and the coolant should look clean.

A malfunctioning thermostat might stick open, which will lengthen engine warm-up time and lower the operating temperature, both of which hamper gas mileage. It could also stick in the closed position, which can cause the engine to overheat. Watch your dashboard coolant temperature gauge as a guide. Even if your car has no gauge but a warning light, one way to discover a malfunctioning thermostat is to pay attention to your car's heater. If it isn't delivering warm air within five minutes, even in freezing weather, get that thermostat checked.

Check belt tensions

Belts that drive the air conditioner, water pump, and power steering pump must be tight enough not to slip, but not so tight as to bind. A rule of thumb used to suggest that belts needed a half-inch of slack, but some of today's engines are more delicate. Their belts must be checked by following the manual's instructions exactly, possibly using a measuring instrument to get tension exactly right. In any case, don't forget to shut off the engine before putting your hand anywhere near a belt!

Inspect the battery

Batteries used to demand water periodically, but most of today's batteries are maintenance-free. What you can still do is inspect the cable terminals for corrosion and cleanliness. That can make the difference between getting an engine to start fast and wasting gas while the engine cranks over too slowly—or not at all.

An engine block heater

Motorists in the south may never give a moment's thought to such a device, but northern dwellers and Canadians know this one well. Many of their cars have the telltale little plug sticking out of the grille. Connect it to ordinary house current and the crankcase stays warm overnight. Not only does the engine turn more freely in the morning, it warms up faster—wasting less fuel during that crucial period.

Pay attention to the brakes

Take note of suspicious symptoms. A dragging brake is not only dangerous, but can drag gas mileage down with every rotation. Brake maintenance is best left to experienced mechanics. But if you feel comfortable putting a corner of the car on the jack, as if to change a tire, give the wheel a spin to see if anything seems to be dragging. And we can all make sure the parking brake is never left on when starting off.

Wheel alignment and tire balance

A professional's equipment is needed to check these, but a misaligned front end or unbalanced tire can rob plenty of mileage.

Is the car pulling to the side? Chances are an alignment is needed. Unless front wheels are pointing ahead properly, the tires might scrub against the pavement and steal fuel by straining the engine. Vibration at various road speeds suggests the need for balancing. An unbalanced tire also soaks up excess gas.

Promises, promises

If there really were a device that could be added to an engine to yield 100 miles per gallon, it wouldn't be advertised on late-night infomercials or in tiny ads in the back of magazines. It would be front-page news.

Gimmicks claiming to boost gas mileage—a fluid, a pill, or a gadget of some sort—pop out of the woodwork whenever fuel supply or fuel costs become an issue. Ads tend to bear a startling resemblance to those for "miracle cures" promised by medical charlatans.

The EPA has evaluated more than 100 such "amazing devices" over the years. Only a half dozen produced a "statistically significant increase in fuel economy," and a couple of others did so only by harming emissions. Recall the basic money-saving maxim: If it sounds too good to be true, it is.

In addition to the questionable fuel and oil additives that promise miraculous mileage, many others are produced by reputable companies and sold at auto parts stores. Useful? Depends on who you ask.

Some experts steer clear of chemicals completely. Others allow that the occasional can of fuel-injector cleaner in the tank might help to keep the injectors clean. Gas-tank additives can also absorb water that comes in with the latest fill-up. Neither result has a direct effect on mileage, however. Basically, a car that's filled with high-quality gasoline and oil shouldn't need any additives to keep it running properly.

Be especially wary of extravagant claims for phenomenal mileage, enhanced power, revived performance, and reduced emissions—often all at the same time.

CHAPTER TWO
DRIVE ECONOMICALLY

Good drivers are smooth drivers, and smooth driving saves fuel. Even minor adjustments in how you drive can result in substantial savings in gas and money.

A calm approach to driving may mean smoother starts and fewer sudden stops—and better mileage.

YOU ARE IN CONTROL

Mind over mpg

We tend to allow our emotions to affect our driving. Elated or angry, calm down before getting behind the wheel. Emotionally intense drivers are a lot more likely to engage in fuel-wasting (and stupidly dangerous) acts: gunning the engine, spinning the wheels, and worse.

Remote starters waste gas

Willing to sacrifice a few minutes of personal comfort to save some gas? Ignore that remote starter.

Remote ignition starters allow you to start your vehicle with the press of a key-fob button while still in the climate-controlled comfort of your house or office. The vehicle idles with the heater or air conditioner running, and you step into a warm or chilled interior. But an idling car gets zero miles per gallon, and one running the air conditioning is gulping down the gas.

The alternative is to bring the vehicle's interior to your desired temperature as you drive, which takes a few minutes but makes better use of the fuel you're burning.

Remote starters have been available through the aftermarket for years and recently have been offered as factory-installed options on some new cars. You'll have to judge for yourself whether a few minutes of personal comfort are worth the waste in fuel and exhaust emissions associated with the use of a remote starter.

FILL 'ER UP

Fill the tank only when needed

No point stopping for gas when there's still plenty in the tank. Let it get down to about one-quarter full. Extra stops waste time, and keeping more fuel than needed in the tank adds unwanted weight to your vehicle. A gallon of gas weighs roughly 6 pounds, and the more weight you haul around, the more fuel you'll burn.

Note that there are important exceptions to this rule. During extremely cold weather, keeping the tank near full minimizes the amount of condensation, or water, that can

Why make more trips to the gas station than necessary? Fill the tank completely and save yourself the extra stops.

form in the tank. Excess condensation can promote fuel-line freeze and other problems.

Other exceptions depend on your personal travel patterns. If you regularly drive long distances, or at odd hours, or in desolate conditions, or in hazardous weather, it's obviously in your interest to keep a generous supply of gas in the tank. Plan for the unexpected.

Buy gas on cool mornings

Liquids, and that includes gasoline, expand when warm. So you actually get a bit more for the same amount of cash by buying gas when it's most dense, even though the pump shows the same total.

Gas up along the way

As a rule, there's no point driving out of your way, or making a special trip, just to save a few cents per gallon. Make the service-station stop part of your regular route.

The exception is during periods of rapid price hikes. Then the difference could amount to more than pennies. So pay attention to current prices in your area, and take note of the stations that offer the best bargains.

Gasoline octane ratings

Octane has nothing to do with a gasoline's quality. The octane figure indicates a fuel's resistance to "knocking." That's the metallic pinging sound you may sometimes hear when accelerating rapidly, or lugging up a hill. Knock may be accompanied by run-on, or dieseling, in which your engine continues to turn over or sputter after you've switched off the ignition. Severe knocking or run-on over an extended period can damage engine parts. Often, as an engine ages, it becomes more sensitive to lower-octane gas.

No advantage is gained by using an octane higher than is necessary to prevent knocking. And today's cars have computerized powertrain controls designed to adjust ignition timing and other engine functions to prevent knocking.

What's the correct octane for your vehicle?

Only a small percentage of vehicles require mid-grade or premium fuel. These are usually sporty or luxury-oriented vehicles with high-performance engines, and those vehicles with turbocharged or supercharged gasoline engines.

It's essential to consult your owner's manual to find out the proper octane level for your vehicle. (Some auto manufacturers also post the octane requirement on a sticker inside the fuel-filler door.)

Note that your owner's manual may list a particular octane level as "recommended" or "required." The "recommended" octane, usually mid-grade or premium, is the one you should choose for "best" performance, the manual will say. Your car will run fine if you choose not to follow that recommendation, and you'll be hard pressed to notice the few horsepower sacrificed to the lower octane. If a particular octane level is required, however, use it.

Most cars don't need high-octane gas. Consult your owner's manual, you may be wasting money.

At the gas pump, a label on the pump displays the octane ratings available at that station. The higher the octane, the more you'll pay. Use the correct octane, and save.

Regular-grade gas is usually rated at 87 octane, midgrade at 89 octane, and premium at 91 or above. The higher the altitude above sea level, the lower the octane requirement, and you'll see this reflected on the pump in octane numbers lower by one or two digits for the same grade of gas available at lower altitudes. Generally, hotter air temperatures and/or lower humidity levels increase the need for higher-octane fuel.

FUEL-EFFICIENT DRIVING

Warm it on the run

Modern engines don't need long warm-up periods, and idling until it warms up wastes gas—an idling engine gets zero mpg, remember—and is mechanically inefficient, too.

When your vehicle has been sitting for more than a few hours, especially in cold weather, simply start off slowly, without gunning the engine or zipping up to highway speeds. This circulates the vehicle's fluids and loosens up mechanical components more efficiently than just idling in place and actually warms the car more quickly.

Easy does it

Accelerate no more forcefully than needed to mesh smoothly into traffic. Fuel consumption is directly related to how hard the engine is working. Ask it to race away from a stop rather than saunter away sensibly, and you'll be visiting the gas station all too frequently. Guaranteed. Ask it to barge up a steep grade rather than feathering the throttle just enough to sustain momentum, and you'll be able to watch the needle on your gas gauge drop.

Even jabbing the accelerator during passing maneuvers or lane changes eats away at fuel economy. On the freeway, zooming up to the traffic ahead, then having to hit your brakes, is a fuel-wasting exercise. The best drivers are smooth drivers.

Lose traction, lose fuel

Even if you're not trying to race away from a stop, you may find your tires slipping, especially on wet surfaces. Each time a tire slips, whatever the cause, you're losing gas mileage as well as essential traction. Take care when starting off on slippery or unpaved roads. Slow down on rough pavement.

rpm and mpg

An engine's workload is determined by how fast the crankshaft is turning. The crankshaft transmits engine power to the transmission and then in turn to the wheels, and crankshaft speed is measured in revolutions per minute, as indicated on a tachometer.

A manual transmission gives the driver full control over rpm because the driver can make the engine speed up or slow down via gear selection. The lower the gear, the higher the rpm. The higher the rpm, the more torque the engine is producing, and the more fuel it is using. Automatic transmissions take some of this control out of the driver's hands, but they, too, can be manipulated to maximize fuel efficiency.

High rpms mean more gas is being burned. Shift into the highest gear possible for best mileage.

Shift smartly

With a manual gearbox, get into the upper gears quickly. Optimal shift points vary, depending on the engine/gearing combination, but for best economy you might need to shift to second by about 15 mph and reach top gear by the time you're traveling 30–35 mph.

Driving "stick" gives you more control of your fuel economy. Avoid staying in lower gears too long for best mileage.

Take advantage of the upshift light

If your manual-transmission car has an upshift indicator, use it as a guide. Using signals from the engine, transmission, and accelerator pedal, the indicator tells you exactly when to upshift to maintain greatest efficiency—thus top economy.

When the engine speed is high compared to the position of the accelerator pedal, the shift indicator lamp signals that you can get the same performance from less fuel by shifting upward without losing power.

Tests conducted by Saab and the EPA compared operation of cars that had an upshift indicator to those that did not. In the EPA city driving test, use of the indicator brought an average gas mileage improvement of more than 9 percent. Even without such an indicator, shift into a higher gear sooner than you normally would and use fifth gear as much as possible to stretch your fuel.

Watch the tachometer

The tachometer allows you to find the engine's most efficient rpm and stay close to that point whenever feasible. What speed is that?

The exact figure depends on the engine but is typically the speed at which it produces the greatest torque output. For economy's sake, it's generally wise to remain below 3,000 rpm—possibly below 2,000—most of the time and to shift into the next gear before the engine gets much beyond its optimum rpm level. Naturally, too low an engine speed does nothing for economy, so running below 1,500 or so isn't ordinarily a good idea.

Skip an occasional gear

No rule says you have to use each gear of your manual transmission every time, going through a never-changing 1–2–3–4–5 sequence. Try going directly from first to third (skipping second); or go from second to fourth without using third. This technique is especially useful if heavy traffic has caused you to rev too high in the lower gear already, as when merging into an expressway from the entry lane.

Get the most from your automatic transmission

An automatic transmission liberates you from shifting gears yourself, but nothing is free, and an engine must work a little harder, and use a bit more gas, to transmit power through an automatic transmission than a manual. For proof, look no further than EPA fuel economy estimates, which are invariably lower for an automatic transmission than for that same vehicle equipped with a manual.

Still, there are some things you can do to maximize fuel efficiency in an automatic-transmission vehicle.

During acceleration, listen as the engine note rises, then falls, to get a sense of when the transmission is reaching the "top" of one gear ratio and changing down to the next, lower ratio. Also, watch the needle on the tachometer climb up the rpm range and descend correspondingly. Remember, the higher the rpm, the more fuel you're burning.

Some automatic transmissions tend to stay in lower gears a little too long for peak economy. You can sometimes coax the transmission into shifting to high gear earlier than normal by letting up on the gas as you pass 30 mph or so. Then, once it's in top gear, continue to accelerate very gradually.

That little OD light

Virtually all manual and automatic transmissions have an overdrive gear that can be employed to save fuel. It's usually the highest-numbered gear and lets the engine run at a slower speed while the car maintains a given road speed.

If you're looking to save gas, get into an overdrive gear as soon as possible and stay there until you need the extra power afforded by a lower gear.

With an automatic transmission, a lot of that decision-making is out of your hands. Automatics tend to move to the highest gear on their own, precisely to save fuel. But in some vehicles you can shift into and out of overdrive. Usually, it's done via a button on the shift lever. Typically, an "OD" light illuminates in the instrument panel when an automatic is shifted into overdrive. If you have inadvertently shifted out of overdrive, press the button to get back in for optimal fuel economy.

Many modern automatic transmissions allow drivers to change gears manually by moving the shift lever through a separate gate. This doesn't duplicate the degree of gear control afforded by a manual transmission, but it will allow you to select a lower gear for more throttle response. Doing so increases engine rpm and burns more gas. For best fuel efficiency, shift into the highest gear whenever possible, or simply shift into Drive and let the automatic do what it's designed to: select the most economical gear at each step of the way.

Make sure nothing's afoot

Don't drive with a foot resting on the brake pedal, however lightly. Even the slightest application of your brakes while in motion will drag down fuel economy. It'll place an unnecessary burden on the other powertrain components, and you'll wear out your brakes rapidly, as well.

SAVING GAS WHILE SITTING STILL

Shift to neutral when stopped

If you're not moving but your engine is running, you're getting zero miles per gallon. Idling at a traffic light is a fuel-economy killer, as is waiting to clear a construction zone, or sitting while a freight train crawls by. And there's a good reason our most frustrating traffic condition is called stop-and-go-driving.

Notice that shifting your automatic or manual transmission into neutral calms down your engine and drops the rpm. That saves gas. Shift into neutral even for a long traffic light.

Keeping an automatic transmission in "Drive" puts an extra load on it, which drains away fuel. In neutral, it's resting—or at least, as close to rest as an automatic ever gets. This shift is even more important when the air conditioner is running, so the engine doesn't have to strain so hard at idle.

Shut off the engine when stopped for a while

Even when stopped for a mile-long freight train, a lot of drivers keep their engines running. A minute of idling consumes more gas than a restart.

So whenever you expect to be stopped for a minute or more, shut off the ignition. No, not at every red light, though some experts advise that even a 30-second stop is worth a shutdown. Use your judgment, but when standing in a bank drive-up line, or at a fast food carryout, if it looks like a long wait without moving, turn off that engine.

Note that many gas/electric hybrid vehicles (discussed in the Buying Economically section in the next chapter) automatically shut off the gas engine in most conditions if the vehicle is stopped for even a few seconds. They restart instantly when the gas pedal is applied. The engineers who designed those hybrids know the fuel-saving value of engine shutoff.

Don't race the engine at stoplights

It's hard to understand why people are so inclined to tromp on the pedal—sometimes every couple of seconds—while waiting for the green. What's to be gained, except drawing attention to yourself?

If you need to pump the pedal to keep the engine from dying, chances are fuel economy isn't your major worry and you need to consult a mechanic.

Hang on with the brake on an upgrade

While at a stoplight or stop sign on an inclined pavement, keep the car from drifting backward by pressing on the brake pedal in the normal manner. Don't use the clutch or automatic transmission to keep from sliding back. You'd be wasting fuel as well as putting a strain on the components.

Shut down when you leave the car

If it's a good idea to shut off the engine when stopped for more than a minute while you're still in the driver's seat, obviously it's *essential* to do so when you're stopping for a while and getting out. Don't let the engine idle while making a phone call, hopping into a store, or dropping off the dry cleaning. Sure, that might keep the interior warm in winter or cool in summer, but the gasoline is just sloshing through, accomplishing no useful purpose. To say nothing of the fact that an idling car is just begging for a thief to take it away.

Park it now

If you're a city dweller, you'll never find that perfect, once-in-a-lifetime parking spot. Why try? Don't waste time and fuel cruising for an ideal spot, steps away from your destination. Pick the one that comes along first, even if it means walking a few blocks. The exercise will do you good.

In a similar vein, park so you don't have to move your vehicle a short time later. Don't leave it sitting on the street or in the driveway just to move into the garage later. By that time, the engine has cooled down and you're wasting gas just to start briefly—as well as putting undo wear on the engine.

Don't rev the engine before shutting off the ignition

Many of us learned to do this on carburetor-equipped engines, in the belief that stomping the gas as we turned off the switch would "prime" the carb (put a jolt of gasoline in its bowl). Most of the time, it did little or no good.

For today's fuel-injected engines, it's a complete waste of fuel. Not only that, the final spurt of raw gasoline winds up dumped on the cylinder walls where it can wash away the essential lubricant, paving the way for increased wear.

ACCESSORIES AND OTHER TRICKS

Don't flip that switch!

Nearly every option, every accessory on the car carries a penalty in gas mileage. Why? To start with, every one adds weight: maybe a little, maybe a lot, but every pound to be hauled demands a little more fuel to do the job. Secondly, most of those convenience extras operate on electricity, and electricity in a car—like in a home—comes at a price. That price is fuel consumption.

Take care with air

The impact on fuel economy of accessories such as heated seats or a high-powered audio system is measured in tenths of a mile per gallon. The air conditioner can knock mileage down by whole units.

The compressor that runs your vehicle's air conditioner demands a huge amount of energy, which puts a drain on the engine. However, use of the air conditioner doesn't always result in a dramatic drop in fuel mileage. Sometimes, using the air conditioner saves fuel.

Running the A/C in stop-and-go-traffic can cost you up to 4 mpg because the engine simply isn't being revved enough to offset the load placed on it by the compressor. On the highway, as the engine is already turning at a low-stress rpm, the fuel costs associated with A/C are far less extreme.

And as you approach the speed limit, it can actually be cheaper to run the air conditioner than to open the windows. How come? Because open windows create severe aerodynamic drag as the vehicles body tries to glide through the air.

The trade-off between open windows and running the A/C tips at about 50 mph. Below that you're generally better off with the windows open. Above that, running the A/C will actually save you fuel.

To save fuel any time you run the A/C, set the temperature control somewhere above frigid cold. That keeps the compressor from running virtually constantly. Use your climate system's economy setting, or a warmer level on the temperature selector.

Close the windows, open the vents

Instead of making a choice between air conditioning and open windows on the road, you could simply rely on the car's ventilation system. Just open one or two windows a crack.

Except on really stifling days, or when moving slowly through traffic, it might keep the car nearly as cool as with "air." Not every modern car's vents deliver a suitably cool breeze, unfortunately. Study your owner's manual to see how your system works best. For such a simple notion, some systems are surprisingly complex, with a bewildering selection of fresh-air flow possibilities. Opening the rear windows, or a minivan's rear vents, helps airflow.

Headlights and fuel economy

We're proponents of seeing and being seen while driving, and that means liberal use of headlights. To be seen by other drivers, we advise switching headlights on at the hint of dusk, or in even slightly overcast conditions. And we use them on twisty country roads no matter the light conditions.

Some vehicles, notably those from General Motors, take care of that for you with daytime running lights (DRLs). These illuminate the headlamps anytime the ignition is switched on. Safety studies show DRLs make vehicles more visible to other drivers, and nearly all published reports indicate DRLs reduce multiple-vehicle daytime crashes.

Of course, headlights draw electrical power, and generating that power burns some fuel. But the National Highway Traffic Safety Administration estimates DRLs cost just a fraction of a mile per gallon, depending on the type of system used. Most DRLs operate headlamps at less than normal power during daylight hours, thereby conserving energy and reducing the effect on a vehicle's fuel economy.

Granted, running headlights other than just at nighttime can shorten bulb life. But whether you switch them on yourself or drive a vehicle equipped with DRLs, we're talking a few dollars per year in extra fuel costs and bulb-replacement expenses. That's a small price to pay for the added safety.

Use cruise control prudently

This often-misunderstood device can save gas when operated properly, at the correct times—or it can become a wastrel when used foolishly.

"Cruise" is just the ticket for driving those long, flat stretches. Not only can you relax your right foot and not worry about the speedometer reading, but it often keeps speed steadier than you can manage manually. And what does steady speed bring? That's right, better gas mileage.

Now the bad news. In hilly terrain, where the unit has to keep increasing and decreasing speed, it can eat into mileage. On slippery pavement, the last thing you want is cruise control, which doesn't detect wheel slippage and will likely try to speed up at times when safety demands that the car slow down.

Why does it start to guzzle when the going gets tough?

When heading up a hill or resuming speed after tapping the unit off, it virtually floors the accelerator to get back up to speed. Remember—for maximum economy, we want steady, gradual speed changes. Conversely, the cruise control option slows the engine too much when going downhill, holding the car back. Used with discretion, then, cruise control is a marvelous convenience; left on too often for too long, it drains away all the gain.

Turn off the high-draw accessories

After turning off the engine, switch off the heater motor, air conditioner, and any other accessory that demands high current. That way, they won't go into action the instant you start the car next. After all, that heater won't do any good until the engine is warmed up again, so why have its blower running for nothing?

Going on a long trip? On level highways, cruise control will maintain an efficient constant speed better than your right foot can.

Some accessories draw much more power than others, of course. Rear defrosters demand plenty, which is why they include an automatic shutoff in case you forget.

CHAPTER THREE
SUVS AND MPG

Buoyed in great measure by affordable fuel, America in the 1990s turned its automotive appetite to light trucks. The category includes pickups, minivans, and the models that experienced the fastest-rising popularity of all—sport-utility vehicles.

A HUNGER FOR SUVS

In 1980, light-duty trucks accounted for just 12 percent of new-vehicle sales. The share was 31 percent by 1990 and reached a high of 54 percent in mid 2004. For SUVs, the share of the U.S. new-vehicle market was just 10 percent in 1994. By 2004, it was 24 percent.

Light-truck sales didn't slip as gas prices rose during 2005, though SUV buyers did begin to switch from thirsty truck-based wagons, such as the Chevrolet Tahoe and Ford Explorer, to lighter-weight and thriftier car-type SUVs, such as the Chevy Equinox and Honda Pilot.

Ford Edge is typical of the recent crop of "crossover" SUVs. Crossovers tend to ride and handle better than the truck-type SUVs—and use less fuel.

Even after the price shocks following Hurricane Katrina in September 2005, light trucks still were outselling cars, but the lead had shrunk to 51 percent of the market. And sales of large, truck-type SUVs continued to shrink in favor of car-type crossover models.

But it was at $3.50 per gallon that truck shopping definitively subsided, and at $4.00 pickup truck and SUV sales languished. This was good news for anyone shopping for a large truck, as rebates and other incentives made for some impressive bargains.

As a category, light trucks average about 25 percent less fuel economy than passenger cars. Within light trucks, the miles-per-gallon spectrum starts with full-size pickups and SUVs as the least efficient, followed by truck-type midsize SUVs, with compact and car-based SUVs the most efficient.

Buying with fuel economy in mind

In general, we urge potential SUV buyers to consider their purchase rationally, not emotionally. Sure, SUVs are trendy, and their high ride height and sheer size afford a sense of security. But that ride height requires you to climb, not step, in and out. And tall-riding vehicles are more prone to rollover accidents. Minivans offer more usable interior space than any large SUV, and many station wagons afford nearly as much cargo room as a midsize SUV and more than most compacts. The added traction of all-wheel-drive is also available in vehicles that are not SUVs.

But if you're committed to an SUV, here's our advice. If you regularly tow a trailer of more than 5,000 pounds, you need the stout truck-type frame and burly V8 engine that's the bread and butter of the truck-type SUV. And if you frequently travel in severe off-road conditions, the truck-type frame might also serve you well.

But for every other use to which the vast majority of Americans put an SUV, a car-type crossover SUV is the more sensible, and fuel-smart, choice. They ride and handle better, offer a range of 4-cylinder and V6 powertrains, and most AWD versions do reasonably well off pavement, too.

Go about picking a fuel-efficient SUV in much the same way you would a frugal car—without expecting as thrifty a result, of course. Consider the choice of available engines and transmissions, and go easy on the weight-adding options.

Nix 4WD if economy is your goal

Four-wheel drive has its good points, but fuel economy is not ordinarily among them. EPA estimates and Consumer Guide® road test results illustrate the difference. The extra drive train components just add too much weight, so even discreet use of 4WD carries a big penalty every day, whether it's engaged or not. Not every 4WD vehicle qualifies as an out-and-out guzzler; but unless statistics suggest otherwise, assume that you'll pay always for off-road and foul-weather capability you'll use only sometimes.

If you don't need the off-road traction versatility of true 4WD, all-wheel drive is an attractive alternative. These systems are lighter in weight than 4WD and actually are more useful on-road because, unlike 4WD, they generally require no action from the driver to deliver power to all four wheels. Some systems also offer low-range gearing and other off-pavement traction aids.

HYBRIDS AND DIESELS

Gas/electric hybrids

Gas/electric hybrid vehicles combine the benefits of gasoline engines and electric motors and can be configured to obtain different objectives, such as improved fuel economy, increased power, or additional auxiliary power for electronic devices and power tools. None of the hybrid cars and trucks on sale in the U.S. requires plug-in charging—yet. Expect to see plug-in hybrids in showrooms by 2011. The current generation of hybrid vehicles instead uses a combination of the gas engine's power and systems that "recapture" otherwise-lost energy (mostly from braking) to recharge the motor's batteries.

Its shape has become synonymous with frugality. Prius is now one of Toyota's best selling cars.

As touched on in the "EPA vs. real-world mpg" section, gas/electric hybrids tend to get better fuel economy in city driving than in highway use.

Think diesel once again

Motorists who were "burned" by the last wave of diesel power, in the late 1970s and early '80s, probably wouldn't buy one on a bet. By now, everybody's heard about the reliability problems of General Motors's diesel V8s, in particular, and the inadequacy of most smaller diesels as well.

For economy, however, the diesel engine is hard to beat, delivering as much as 25 percent more mileage (on diesel fuel) than a gasoline engine of similar size. Only a handful of diesels remained available through the 1980s, but Mercedes-Benz and Volkswagen are leading a diesel resurgence—with engines far superior to earlier versions in smoothness, quietness, and overall performance.

DON'T NEGLECT THE USED-CAR SIDE

Selecting a miserly *used* car

Two out of every three cars purchased are used, and the variances in fuel economy are vast. Most of the rules for selecting a secondhand vehicle are the same as for a new one: pick a car with a limited number of power-draining options, select the smallest model that works for you, and so on.

Get rid of that old clunker

More than 37 million cars over 10 years old remain on the road. Only a fraction of these are historic or collectible vehicles that need to be protected. Another handful is kept in pristine shape, driven moderately, causing little harm. All too many of the balance, however, are clunkers that pollute the air and guzzle more than their share of fuel. Worse yet, they're all too likely to be poorly maintained, incapable of operating even within the looser limits of the era in which they were built. Do us all a favor: Kill that wasteful clunker.

BUYING ECONOMICALLY

More to it than simple self-interest

From the mid 1970s to 1990, the average fuel economy for all vehicles on the road in the U.S. doubled from about 14 to 28 mpg. By 2005, it had dropped to 24 mpg.

Driving a fuel-efficient vehicle will save you gas money, of course, but such a decision has other, broader, implications.

Nature required more than 200 million years to develop all of the oil below the earth's surface. Mankind required just 200 years to consume half that. If current rates of consumption continue, the U.S. Department of Energy says, the world's remaining resources of conventional oil will be exhausted in 40 years.

About 60 percent of the oil the world consumes powers transportation vehicles, and half of that goes to passenger cars and light trucks.

As oil resources dwindle and oil becomes prohibitively expensive to locate and extract, mankind will replace petroleum as a primary source of power because alternative forms of energy simply will be more economical.

Still, burning less gas in our vehicles will affect the pace at which oil is consumed. Perhaps more important, fuel conservation will impact the demand for oil. And that has meaningful political, technological, and environmental consequences.

Dependence on imported oil

Transportation accounts for two-thirds of U.S. petroleum use, and America depends on imports for more than half of its oil. As domestic resources are used up, dependence on foreign oil will increase. Some 70 percent of the world's oil reserves are in the Middle East, under control of the Organization of the Oil Producing Companies (OPEC) oil cartel.

Burgeoning middle classes in India and China have driven up demand for gasoline. In the U.S. about half of all oil becomes gas. Much of the rest becomes diesel fuel.

In the past, the dependence on oil has had a profound effect on the U.S. economy. The department of energy calculates that oil price shocks and price manipulation by the OPEC cartel from 1979 to 2000 cost the U.S. economy about $7 trillion, almost as much as we spent on national defense over the same period.

With increasing world dependence on OPEC oil, future price shocks are possible. Each major oil price shock of the past 30 years was followed by an economic recession in the United States.

One camp insists technological progress holds the solution to oil dependence. Our attention should be on developing energy-efficient vehicle technologies and fresh energy sources to replace petroleum cleanly and inexpensively.

Another approach places an emphasis on conservation. Curbing our demand for petroleum will help reduce U.S. oil dependence and provide an incentive for auto manufacturers to produce cleaner, better running, and more energy-efficient vehicles.

The environmental element

In any discussion of the environmental responsibility shouldered by the United States, it is important to recognize that the U.S. accounts for 25 percent of the world's economic output.

That said, here goes.

More than one-third of the oil shipped by sea is destined for the United States. Air pollution is a worldwide problem, and the U.S. is the largest emitter of manmade greenhouse gases, accounting for 20 percent of all manmade greenhouse emissions.

Reduce demand for imported oil, and less will be shipped by sea, with the prospect of fewer oil spills.

Transportation vehicles produce most of the key chemicals that pollute the air, causing smog and health problems. Air quality is poorest in developing industrial nations, but almost 150 million Americans live in areas that fail at least one National Ambient Air Quality standard. Vehicles with higher fuel economy may produce less pollution over time than vehicles with lower fuel economy.

mpg and do-re-me

The auto editors of Consumer Guide® road test more than 200 new cars, trucks, minivans, and SUVs per year. We drive these vehicles the way their owners would: urban commuting, suburban shopping, and interstate travel. We keep scrupulous fuel-economy records on each vehicle.

In real-world driving, the 8-cylinder SUVs we test average about 13 mpg in city/highway driving. The average is about 16 mpg for 6-cylinder SUVs and minivans and about the same for most luxury cars. The typical midsize car we test gets approximately 22 mpg, the typical 4-cylinder compact car comes in closer to 25 mpg.

Later in this section, we'll discuss the gap between EPA fuel-economy estimates and real-world fuel consumption. For now, let's talk about how much your choice of vehicle type affects what you'll shell out for gas.

The math is pretty simple. The average American drives more than 12,000 miles a year. At $4.00 a gallon, we're spending, on average, $250 a month on fuel.

According to the American Automobile Association, the average price for a gallon of unleaded regular gas nationally in May 2004 was $1.84. By August 2005, it was $2.33. By September 2005, in the weeks after Hurricane Katrina, the pump price for regular was $3.04. As shocking as $3.00-a-gallon was, it proved just a primer for the $4.00 pump prices seen by the summer of 2008.

Owners tend to keep a new vehicle an average of seven years. The typical American vehicle racks up about 12,000 miles per year. Using the real-world fuel-economy averages as recorded by Consumer Guide® and the average price of gas as of May 2008, here's an idea of how much each of these types of vehicles would cost to fuel at 12,000 miles per year.

Regular-grade fuel at $4.00 per gallon		
	1 Year	7 Years
8-cylinder SUV (13 mpg)	$3,692	$25,844
6-cylinder SUV, minivan (16 mpg)	$3,000	$21,000
midsize car (22 mpg)	$2,182	$15,274
compact car (25 mpg)	$1,920	$13,440
Premium-grade fuel at $4.25 per gallon		
	1 Year	7 Years
luxury car (16 mpg)	$3,188	$22,316

THE CHOICE IS YOURS

Opportunity knocks

Buying with fuel economy in mind doesn't require you to own a vehicle you don't want. Rather, it means shopping for the vehicle that gives the features you want with the best available fuel economy.

You'll save money on gas and do your part to signal auto manufacturers to make more energy-efficient vehicles.

Your first decision is what *type* of vehicle you'll drive. Choices range from gas-sipping sub compacts to gas-guzzling SUVs, and in between is a bewildering range of cars, trucks, and crossovers.

This basic decision is based on a variety of factors: how much you are able or willing to spend on a vehicle, what size or type of vehicle you may actually require, and the emotional component.

In a very real sense, the opportunity for greatest gas savings rests with those whose economic circumstances give them the freedom to choose from a wider variety of vehicle types. If a tight budget is your guide, you may be forced into a smaller, less-expensive car. That means a relatively lightweight vehicle with few gas-draining options and likely a small, more efficient engine.

If you're in a position to choose from among various sizes and types of vehicles, remember that there are fuel-efficient choices even among seeming gas-guzzlers such as sports cars, premium sedans, and SUVs.

Emotion is part of the fabric of the auto world. What your choice of vehicle says about you, what you think it says about you, and how it makes you feel are at the root of more car-buying decisions than many of us might like to admit. But saving fuel is just as emotional, for what it says about you, and how it makes you feel.

Consumer Guide®'s fuel-economy experience

Here are representative samples of some of the most fuel-efficient 2008 models in several vehicle categories as recorded in road tests by the auto editors of Consumer Guide®. For an up-to-the-minute look at the fuel economy we recorded for hundreds of new and used cars, go to consumerguide.com.

Note: Though it would be impossible to drive each vehicle in the same manner and conditions, efforts are made to balance the ratio of city and highway driving. We present these numbers for comparison only. Your mileage may differ significantly.

SUBCOMPACT CAR:

Hyundai Accent 34.2 mpg

Our test hatchback had the standard five speed manual transmission. Though no ball of fire, Accent is far more refined than most shoppers would expect.

Pros:

- Better than 30 mpg
- Standard front side and curtain side airbags
- Tidy size makes for easy maneuvering

Cons:

- Lacks power for confident merging and passing
- Noisy engine
- Limited rear-seat space

Best Value:

We recommend the GLS sedan with manual transmission and available antilock brakes. The available Popular Equipment package adds a lot of good stuff for not much extra.

COMPACT CAR:

Honda Civic Hybrid 45.7 mpg

Currently Honda's only hybrid model, Civic Hybrid is about the stingiest car available in the U.S. It's also relatively fun to drive.

Pros:

- Better than 40 mpg
- Loaded with standard safety equipment
- Impressive fit and finish

Cons:

- Only adequate power
- Rear seat tight for adults
- Noisy engine

Best Value:

There is only one Civic Hybrid model, and it comes loaded. Huge demand means dealers are charging a premium over sticker price. Shop carefully.

MIDSIZE CAR:

Kia Rondo 20.5 mpg

This roomy, refined seven-passenger wagon can do almost everything a midsize SUV can do except tow. It deserves a space on every frugal family's shopping list.

Pros:

- Better than 20 mpg with available V6
- Class-leading passenger and cargo space
- Impressive array of standard safety features

Cons:

- Lackluster power from available four-cylinder engine
- Even V6 lacks surplus passing punch
- Lack of available all-wheel drive

Best Value:

Go with the loaded EX V6. Even fully optioned with leather seating for seven, this high-value family mover lists for less than $25,000.

MIDSIZE CAR:

Mazda5 22.0 mpg

Think of Mazda5 as a Kia Rondo with sliding side doors. Our test car came with the automatic transmission. Shifting for yourself would result in an even thriftier ride.

Pros:

- Better than 20 mpg
- Class-exclusive sliding side doors
- Seven-passenger seating

Cons:

- Four-cylinder is only engine; power just adequate
- Engine noise
- Third-row seats best reserved for youngsters

Best Value:

The mid-line Touring model represents the best Mazda5 value. Still a top-line Grand Touring, even loaded, comes in around $28,000—not a lot for a roomy, three-row family vehicle.

LARGE CAR:

Dodge Charger 19.4 mpg

Skip the thirsty HEMI V8 and go for the midline V6. Charger offers plenty of adult cabin space, a sporty profile, and reasonable thrift.

Pros:

- Almost 20 mpg
- Good power from the 3.5-liter V6
- Impressive ride and handling

Cons:

- Cabin materials look budget grade
- Incautious options selections can raise price alarmingly
- Small trunk opening

Best Value:

A carefully optioned SXT is the strongest value in the Charger line. Available all-wheel drive is a boon to snow-belt dwellers, though it costs more and hurts fuel economy.

LARGE CAR:

Mercury Sable 20.3 mpg

Roomy and smart-handling, this slow-selling sedan is always available with lavish rebates and deep discounts. Apart from styling and equipment, Sable is identical to the similarly frugal Ford Taurus.

Pros:

- Better than 20 mpg
- Impressive ride and handling
- Spacious cabin

Cons:

- Antiskid system only available on top-line Limited
- Confusing audio controls
- Anonymous styling

Best Value:

Opt for the Limited with few extra options. An overloaded Sable can break the $35,000 barrier. Like the Dodge Charger, Sable can be had with all-wheel drive.

COMPACT SUV:

Saturn Vue Hybrid 31.6 mpg

This refined hybrid takes the sting out of stinginess. Note that all-wheel drive isn't available on this frugal SUV and that power-hungry drivers will want to look elsewhere.

Pros:

- Better than 30 mpg
- Luxury-level interior accommodations
- Smooth ride

Cons:

- Low on power
- No available third-row seating
- Many Vue options unavailable on Hybrid

Best Value:

A Comfort and Convenience Package is the only option for Vue Hybrid, and we recommend it. Expect most Hybrids in dealer stock to have the package.

MIDSIZE SUV:

Mercedes-Benz ML320 CDI 22.2 mpg

This diesel-powered Mercedes is smooth and strong. Though expensive by absolute standards, the diesel version of this midsize SUV costs just $1000 more than the base model.

Pros:

- Better than 20 mpg
- Abundant power
- Luxury accommodations

Cons:

- Diesel fuel not available at all gas stations
- Diesel fuel costlier than gas, partially offsetting savings
- Diesel regular service costlier than for gasoline models

Best Value:

The ML320 CDI can be equipped like any other M-Class Mercedes, which means that adding $15,000 in options is possible. Skip the roof rack; it can lower fuel economy.

LARGE SUV:

Chevrolet Tahoe Hybrid 22.8 mpg

You pay a lot extra for the Hybrid, but this muscular miser can tow more than 6000 pounds. Our 22.8 mpg results were observed in a rear-drive model.

Pros:

- Better than 20 mpg
- Ample power for passing, merging, towing
- Vast passenger and cargo accommodations

Cons:

- Hybrid only comes loaded, and pricey
- Reduced towing capacity verses conventional Tahoe
- Obnoxious quantity of Hybrid badges and appliqués

Best Value:

Sadly, Chevy only sells the Tahoe Hybrid one way: loaded. Tahoe Hybrid is available with all-wheel drive, though the system will cost you 1–2 mpg.

MINIVAN:
Chrysler Town & Country 18.7 mpg

Our test van came with the biggest engine and loaded with options. Thank clever engineering and Chrysler's six-speed automatic transmission for our impressive mileage.

Pros:

- Nearly 20 mpg
- Good power, smoothly delivered
- Ultra-family-friendly accommodations

Cons:

- Tempting options raise prices fast
- As big as it looks—complicating parking-lot maneuvers
- Cabin finished in relatively cheap-looking plastics

Best Value:

The excellent 4.0-liter V6 comes only in the top-line Limited. Despite the price, it's our pick for overall value. We highly recommend the power-folding third-row seat.

PICKUP TRUCK:
Honda Ridgeline 18.3 mpg

Somewhere between compact and full-size pickups is the Ridgeline. This capable Honda is not especially brawny, but for most truck owners, it's all they really need.

Pros:

- Nearly 20 mpg
- Surprising power from standard V6
- Useful weather-tight cargo-bed storage well

Cons:

- Limited towing capability
- Limited off-road capability
- Cabin finished in relatively cheap-looking plastics

Best Value:

Ridgeline comes only with all-wheel drive. We think the midlevel RTS model offers the best blend of value and passenger comfort.

HYBRID:

Toyota Prius: 45.2 mpg

Prius is the sole hybrid-only vehicle available in the U.S. It's a little slow, and the hybrid system is less than smooth, but no car this roomy uses so little gas.

Pros:

- More than 40 mpg
- Room for four adults, five in a pinch
- Comfortable ride

Cons:

- Wants for power
- Engine noise
- Mushy handling

Best Value:

Any Prius represents a good value, but we recommend avoiding overloaded Touring models with too many options. Dealers are charging a premium right now, so don't count on striking a deal.

SIZE AND SAFETY

lbs vs. mpg

Vehicle weight is the biggest single enemy of fuel economy. A heavy vehicle simply needs more power than a smaller one to produce comparable acceleration and load-hauling capacity. And that's usually achieved by a larger-displacement engine.

Consumer Guide® real-world fuel-economy tests show that for the same model of vehicle, the version equipped with the larger engine almost always uses more fuel than one with the engine that has fewer cylinders or less displacement.

However, in some SUVs and pickup trucks we've tested, the version with the smaller engine averages fewer miles per gallon. In large, heavy vehicles, a larger engine that doesn't have to strain as much can turn out to be more fuel-efficient than the smaller engine choice.

Generally, the larger a vehicle's size, the more it weighs. That isn't an ironclad rule, however. Midsize models loaded with luxury amenities or special-purpose equipment can easily outweigh modestly equipped full-size versions of the same type of vehicle.

Also affecting weight is the job a vehicle is designed to do. Heavy trailer towing or severe off-road capability, for example, may require a beefy frame and reinforced suspension components. Those add weight. Convertibles weigh more than their coupe counterparts. And of vehicles within the same model line, those brimming with safety and convenience items—be they standard features or factory options—weigh noticeably more than their less-well-outfitted siblings.

Size, weight, and safety

Simple laws of physics sometimes dictate truths that are hard to swallow when your aim is to save fuel.

Large, heavy vehicles have lower real-world fatality rates than smaller, lighter vehicles. But it is not possible to simply conclude that size equals safety. That's because some large vehicles, such as full-size pickup trucks, have higher fatality rates than some categories of passenger vehicles, such as full-size sedans and minivans that are not as large or as heavy. Much depends on a vehicle's design, the safety features with which it is equipped, and, not least, its driver demographics.

Fatality rates are generally measured in deaths per 1 million registered vehicles. The ranking of vehicle type by fatality rate can change year to year, depending on variances in reporting and record-keeping. But in general, here is how the vehicle types tend to rank, *listed from lowest fatality rate to highest:*

- Minivans and large cars
- Large SUVs
- Midsize cars
- Midsize SUVs
- Large pickup trucks
- Compact SUVs
- Compact cars
- Compact pickup trucks

A closer look

As you think about the trade-offs between fuel economy and vehicle size, here's a look at some factors that influence the fatality rates of the different types of vehicles.

Minivans tend to be family vehicles and are driven conservatively by a mature, experienced driver population. The same holds true for large cars. Both have generous crush zones and tend to be equipped with such important safety features as curtain side airbags. And neither is at a pronounced size disadvantage.

Large SUVs have size and weight on their side and are built on sturdy truck frames. That frame enhances their passive crash protection, though this rigid metal understructure, combined with the tall ride height of a full-size SUV, means these vehicles can be deadly to occupants of smaller vehicles in a crash. Large SUVs are not inexpensive and so tend to be driven by a mature driver population, as well.

The midsize-car category covers the widest range of models, from bargain-priced sedans to luxury/performance models. They have a low center of gravity that resists rollover accidents and can be equipped with the latest safety features. But their modest size means that they begin to be vulnerable in collisions with larger vehicles, and their diverse owner population includes younger, inexperienced drivers.

Midsize SUVs also cover a broad range of prices, safety equipment, and driver demographics.

Large pickup trucks share many of the same vehicle characteristics as large SUVs, primarily ride height and a heavy frame. But the pickup-truck driver population tends to be younger and less family oriented. It's a higher-risk demographic that drives less prudently, an important factor in the most deadly type of accident affecting trucks and SUVs: the rollover.

Vehicles with a high center of gravity are less stable in changes of direction and have the highest incidence of rollover accidents. A prime cause of death in rollovers is ejection from the vehicle. Pickup drivers, statistically, wear seatbelts less than drivers of any other type of vehicle.

Compact SUVs also have a tall ride height and high incidence of rollovers, plus a relatively inexperienced driver population. And they are of a size and weight that does not give them a decided advantage in passive safety.

Compact cars are light and small, and while some are relatively costly, most are inexpensive transportation for a young, high-risk driving population.

Compact pickup trucks combine the least-desirable safety-related characteristics: relatively small and lightweight; tall center of gravity; high incidence of rollovers; high-risk drivers who tend not to wear seatbelts.

The CAFE debate

Reacting to the 1973–74 Arab Oil Embargo, the federal government in 1975 established Corporate Average Fuel Economy (CAFE) standards that require each automaker's fleet to meet certain gas-mileage thresholds at the risk of monetary penalty.

As of 2008, the required fleet average was 27.5 miles per gallon for passenger cars and 22.5 mpg for light trucks, including SUVs and pickups below 8500 pounds gross vehicle weight. The light-truck target rises to 23.5 mpg in 2010. Legislation under consideration now would raise the standard for all passenger vehicles, car and truck, to 35 mpg by 2020.

CAFE regulations have been credited with saving billions of gallons of gas over the years. Proponents of higher standards say the required averages should be increased more than those already proposed in order to reduce America's fuel consumption and to benefit the environment.

An opposing argument holds that stricter CAFE regulations would force Americans into smaller, lighter vehicles, to the detriment of occupant safety. Some opponents also say a broad increase in fuel economy would reduce the demand for fuel and therefore its price. Americans would drive more miles, negating the intent of the more stringent regulations.

THE COMPLEX ISSUE OF THE EPA AND MPG

The required information

Manufacturers are required by law to post their vehicles' fuel-economy ratings, as certified by the federal Environmental Protection Agency (EPA), on the window stickers of most every new vehicle sold in the U.S. The exception is for vehicles having gross-vehicle-weight ratings over 8,500 pounds, heavy-duty pickups and big SUVs, for example.

The posted information lists the mpg estimate for city driving and for highway driving and also estimates the fuel economy range that most drivers achieve with that particular model.

For a listing of EPA estimates for all vehicles covered by the program, visit www.fueleconomy.gov.

As most of us can attest, these "official" ratings rarely reflect our own real-world driving experience. Fuel economy is not a fixed number. Depending on what, how, and where you drive, the differences can be pronounced. Your vehicle's fuel economy will almost certainly differ from the EPA's fuel economy rating.

The EPA ratings estimate the mpg a "typical" driver should observe under "typical" city and highway conditions. However, most drivers and driving environments aren't typical, and the factors that affect fuel economy can vary significantly:

- Driver behavior & driving conditions
- Vehicle condition & maintenance
- Variations in fuels
- Inherent variations in vehicles
- Engine break-in

So, the EPA rating is a useful tool for comparing vehicles when car buying, but it may not accurately predict the average mpg you will get.

EPA vs. real-world mpg

The chart on the next page is a sampling of the EPA fuel-economy estimates for a variety of vehicles, and the actual miles-per-gallon averages observed by the auto editors of Consumer Guide® during its road-test program. This road-test program subjects vehicles to a mix of city and highway driving by at least four road-test editors. The cars are tested in the Chicago area and usually accumulate 500–600 miles during the test period.

Note the tendency for the observed fuel-economy numbers to mirror the EPA's city estimates. Among other things, the EPA's test cycle does not allow for waiting in line at drive-through restaurants, flipping through your mail in the driveway with the engine running, or pulling over and idling to make a cell-phone call.

EPA vs. real-world mpg (select models)

2008 Vehicle	EPA City/Hwy	CG Observed
Audi Q7 3.6	14/20	17.1
Cadillac DTS	15/22	18.7
Ford Explorer Sport Trac (V8)	13/20	13.5
Honda Accord (4-cylinder)	22/31	22.2
Infiniti QX56	12/17	12.7
Jeep Commander (5.7-liter V8)	13/17	12.5
Lexus ES350	19/27	19.8
Nissan Frontier (V6)	16/20	14.5
Scion XB (automatic)	22/28	20.0
Smart ForTwo	33/41	38.8
Subaru Tribeca	16/21	14.6
Toyota Prius	48/45	45.2
Toyota Sienna (AWD)	17/21	16.4
Volkswagen New Beetle (manual)	20/28	21.3
Volvo V70	16/24	21.6

How new vehicles are tested

Why do the EPA's numbers almost always seem to be off base, or at least on the low side of reality? It has a lot to do with the way new cars and trucks are evaluated for their energy consumption. While it would seem logical to determine a vehicle's fuel economy by simply filling up the tank, driving it on the road or a test track for a set number of city or highway miles, refilling the tank, and dividing the number of miles driven by the number of gallons consumed, this is not how the experts do it.

In fact, tested vehicles don't reach the pavement at all. Rather, a car or truck's fuel economy is measured under rigidly controlled circumstances in a laboratory using a standardized test that's mandated by federal law. Automakers actually do their own testing and submit the results to the EPA, which reviews the data and confirms about 10 to 15 percent of the ratings itself at the National Vehicles and Fuel Emissions Laboratory.

Each model is tested on what's called a dynamometer, which is like a treadmill for cars. While the engine and transmission drive the wheels, the vehicle never actually moves—just the rollers upon which the wheels are placed. A professional driver runs the vehicle through two standardized driving schedules, one each to simulate city and highway motoring, and ensures he or she is maintaining the mandated pace via a real-time computer display.

The "city" program is designed to replicate an urban rush-hour driving experience in which the vehicle is started with the engine cold and is driven in stop-and-go traffic with frequent idling. The car or truck is driven for 11 miles and makes 23 stops over the course of 31 minutes, with an average speed of 20 mph and a top speed of 56 mph. The "highway" program, on the other hand, is created to emulate rural and interstate freeway driving with a warmed-up engine, making no stops (both of which ensure maximum fuel economy). The vehicle is driven for 10 miles over a period of 12.5 minutes with an average speed of 48 mph and a top speed of 60 mph. Both tests are performed with the vehicle's air conditioning and other accessories turned off.

Throughout the test a hose is connected to the vehicle's tailpipe to collect the engine's exhaust. The amount of carbon that's present in what's spewed from the exhaust system is measured to calculate the amount of fuel burned. The

EPA claims this is more accurate than using a fuel-gauge to physically measure the amount of gasoline that's being burned. Still, the final test figures are adjusted downward, by 10 percent for city driving and 22 percent in highway mileage, to help reflect the differences between what happens in a lab and out on an actual road.

Note that for 2008 new tests were added to the process, with net results being slightly lower—and more realistic—reported estimates.

The EPA and hybrids

Another change to the EPA testing procedure involves hybrid vehicles. Before 2008, there was a well-publicized gap between EPA estimates and experienced fuel economy for owners of hybrid-powered vehicles. The EPA's ratings for hybrid vehicles tended to overstate mileage by a factor of 20 percent or more. This discrepancy was wider yet if a motorist drove primarily on the highway.

Ironically, the results of tests conducted by the EPA of a dozen hybrid cars in its own fleet significantly contradict their posted fuel-economy ratings. According to a report on a government Web site, the best the EPA's fleet could muster was a cumulative average of 44.8 mpg for the current-generation Toyota Prius. While this is certainly admirable fuel economy, it's still far below the cars' pre-2008 EPA rating of 60/51. For 2008 that estimate has been revised to 48/45, reasonably in line with Consumer Guide®'s 45.2 mpg findings.

Discrepancies beyond the lab

In addition to the testing methods used to determine the EPA's ratings, a host of other physical and personal factors contribute to the differences between a vehicle's rated and realized energy consumption. For starters, cars and trucks used for evaluation in the EPA's tests are broken in and are in top mechanical shape. New vehicles don't usually attain their top mileage until they're driven about 3,000 to 5,000 miles, and ill-maintained vehicles will consume more gas than those that are in perfect condition. Even relatively minor upkeep factors such as having incorrect air pressure in the tires can affect your vehicle's fuel economy. Depending on where you live, the particular blend of gasoline sold in your area at a given time of the year may have more or less energy content, which in turn results in better or worse fuel economy. What's more, the EPA claims that even small differences in manufacturing and assembling can cause minor disparities in fuel economy from one otherwise alike model to another.

Also, the cars and trucks subjected to fuel economy testing are "driven" without a full complement of passengers, cargo, and options aboard—all else being equal, the heavier a vehicle is, the more fuel an engine will need to burn in order to reach and maintain a set speed. The vehicles are tested without the air conditioning and other electrical accessories in use, which also tend to put a greater load on the engine and in addition, reduce the vehicle's fuel economy.

Physical factors like trip length, traffic conditions, and the weather affect your mileage. Also, installing exterior accessories like roof racks and cargo carriers that hamper a vehicle's aerodynamics take their toll at the pump—the more aerodynamic "drag" that's placed on a vehicle, the more energy it takes to run it, especially at highway speeds. Lead-footed acceleration, heavy braking, high-speed driving, excessive idling, towing, and engaging four-wheel drive will drain your vehicle's gas tank at a higher-than-average rate. The EPA estimates that jackrabbit starts and sudden stops alone reduce a car or truck's fuel economy by as much as 33 percent at highway speeds and five percent in the city.

Not perfect, but useful

While the EPA's fuel-economy estimates may not be a completely accurate prediction of the kind of mileage you'll register during your daily commute, it's still valid as a source of comparison when you shop for a new vehicle. In addition to city and highway mileage estimates, a new vehicle's price sticker will show the fuel-economy range most drivers can expect to actually achieve with that particular model, the annual estimated fuel cost (based on 15,000 miles per year and a predetermined, though not mentioned, cost per gallon of gas), and the fuel-economy range for other models in its size class. The EPA's estimates for all vehicles can be found in a master list posted at www.fueleconomy.gov, and a printed version can be ordered via the Web site as well.

At the least, by checking this list you can get a relative idea of how one particular car or truck measures up against others in its class, or how one type of vehicle fares, on average, in comparison with others. If, for example, you're comparing two vehicles and one is estimated to get a third better fuel economy than another, you can reasonably expect to pay a third more to keep the latter's gas tank filled, all else being equal. This is also valid for noting the relative efficiency among available engines in a given car or truck's model range.

POWERTRAIN DECISIONS AND FUEL ECONOMY

Engine choices

Common sense suggests that the smallest available engine delivers the best miles per gallon. In the real world, that's not always the case. A powerplant that strains, wheezing out inadequate horsepower and torque for the job, just might send you to the gas pump more often rather than less. To say nothing of the fact that the life of an overworked engine is not usually a long one. So while a four-cylinder engine tends to be more economical than a V6 powering the same car and a V6 is more frugal than a V8, smaller isn't always the wisest choice.

What's needed is the best match between car size/weight and engine output. Too small, and it's often overworked, never realizing its economy potential. Too big, and it guzzles more than necessary to get the job done. To choose between a standard and optional engine, check the EPA ratings and the real-world road tests—not only for mileage figures but for comments on the sufficiency or lack of usable power.

Turbochargers and superchargers

At first glance, a turbo sounds like the high-efficiency choice for both performance and economy. After all, it doesn't drain engine power but makes use of exhaust gases to rotate the high-speed turbine. Better yet, it comes into play only when needed—only when tromping hard on the gas pedal for a quick burst of extra power. That extra jolt sucks up plenty of extra fuel, however, as it shoves an oversized air/fuel charge into the engine. If rarely used, it might not hurt mileage much. But how many people buy a turbo and keep their foot light on the pedal? Superchargers, driven directly by the engine, act as a constant drag and cost a bundle in mileage.

Choose an economical axle ratio

Plenty of buyers never realize there's a choice. Often there isn't, but many pickup trucks and some performance-oriented cars are offered with a selection of ratios. As a rule, the lower the number, the greater its economy potential. That's because it allows the engine to run slower for a given road speed. An "economy" axle has a ratio below 3:1 or so. "Performance" axles, which deliver quicker acceleration and are better suited to towing trailers, might come to more than 4:1. The perfect selection depends on the type of driving you do.

Shift for yourself

A quick glance at the EPA ratings for cars available with a choice of manual and automatic transmissions makes it clear that manual gearboxes are the only choice for peak economy. Seldom does the city-driving estimate for automatic come closer than 2–3 mpg to the manual-shift figure. In some cases, the difference is similar on the highway; other automatics achieve better results, rivaling a "stick" when up to speed. Compare the figures before deciding, but remember that high-mpg with a manual comes only when it's shifted with some expertise.

All-wheel drive

Four-wheel drive and fuel economy were discussed at the beginning of this chapter. But many cars and some minivans are available with all-wheel drive. The AWD system in cars and minivans is intended as an all-weather traction aid and is not designed for off-road duty. Thus, it doesn't have the weighty, heavy-duty componentry of most 4WD and AWD systems in pickup trucks and SUVs.

AWD cars and minivans do tend to use more fuel than their 2-wheel drive counterparts. This is due less to any added drag placed on the powertrain by AWD and more to the 100 to 200 pounds the AWD system adds to the weight of the vehicle. But the fuel-mileage difference isn't pronounced, and while AWD adds to the purchase price of the vehicle, it's well worth considering if you frequently travel wet or snowy roads.

EASY ON THE OPTIONS

Amenities and fuel economy

To some people, comfort is a heated leather seat in the winter. Others take comfort in knowing they're eking out every last mile from each gallon of gas they consume.

Nearly every luxury amenity adds weight and drains power, both of which are the enemies of fuel economy—and performance. You'll either drag down the efficiency of your engine or have to shell out for a larger, less efficient engine designed to shrug off the extra strain placed on it by power convenience features.

Air conditioning

Air conditioning is standard on all but a few low-cost compact cars and trucks. It's a necessity in many parts of the country. And even when the weather isn't sweltering, the ability to drive with windows closed can reduce driver fatigue on long trips or in noisy city traffic.

Still, an air conditioner adds a hundred pounds or so to the car's weight and drains energy even if the switch is never flipped on. In the city, you're talking about as much as

3–4 lost miles per gallon whenever it's used. Can you learn to live without it?

Sunroofs

Just like an open window, an open sunroof compromises a car's ability to slice through the air. And a sunroof's sliding glass or metal panel, electric motor, and the tracks and reinforcements upon which it rides to open and close all add lots of extra weight to your vehicle.

Cruise control

As described earlier in this book, cruise control can boost mileage if it's used properly on long, flat stretches; but it can be a drain on economy if operated carelessly. If you do plenty of highway driving, it may be worth the price in both economy and convenience.

Roof rack

Is it really worth hauling a wind catcher all year long just to have it available during vacation time? If so, try to avoid putting too much bulky stuff up there. An older, non-aero sedan or wagon might not be affected as much as a modern vehicle, in terms of mileage.

Colors

Light colors reflect sunlight and help keep the interior cool. Dark colors do the opposite. Color choice, then, affects the need to use the air conditioner or heater.

Power seats, heated seats, navigation systems—and on and on

Handy, yes; economical, no. Each accessory draws energy or adds weight, decreasing mileage.